SCHOLASTIC

Phonics Picture Puzzles for Little Learners

NEW YORK • TORONTO • LONDON • AUCKLAND • SYDNEY
MEXICO CITY • NEW DELHI • HONG KONG • BUENOS AIRES

Teaching *Resources*

Produced and edited by Immacula A. Rhodes
Cover design by Maria Lilja
Interior design by Kathy Massaro

ISBN: 978-0-545-31881-5

1 2 3 4 5 6 7 8 9 10   40   18 ·17 16 15 14 13 12 11

Contents

▲▲▲▲▲▲▲

Phonics Picture Puzzles
··

Introduction

Phonics Picture Puzzles for Little Learners is a collection of engaging hidden pictures, color-by-sound activities, mazes, and connect-the-dot puzzles that get children excited about learning as they build phonics skills and concepts. More than three dozen irresistible activities offer children lots of practice in identifying initial and final consonant sounds, short and long vowels, diphthongs, variant vowels, *r*-controlled vowels, consonant blends, and digraphs.

Research shows that a strong foundation in phonics is an important component in building reading confidence and fluency. The activities in this book provide children of all learning styles with a motivating, fun way to independently practice and build skills while helping them meet important language arts standards. (See Meeting the Language Arts Standards for more.) The self-checking component provides instant feedback, making the activities ideal for use in learning centers, as independent work or day-starters, for fast-finishers, or homework. For your convenience, an answer key is also included on pages 45–48. No matter how you choose to incorporate the activities in your classroom routine, these puzzles will delight and challenge children while putting them on the path to reading success!

What the Research Says

Phonics instruction focuses on the relationship between sounds and symbols. In his book *Phonics From A to Z*, 2nd ed. (Scholastic, 2006), reading specialist Wiley Blevins notes that the faster children can decode words, and the more words they recognize by sight, the more fluent they become, leaving more time and energy to focus on comprehension (Freedman and Calfee, 1984; LaBerge and Samuels, 1974). Blevins cites Cunningham's (1995) observation that the brain works as a "pattern detector." Since blends, digraphs, and many vowel sounds contain reliable sound-spelling patterns, learning to recognize their common patterns increases and improves word recognition skills.

How to Use This Book

Each delightful puzzle is designed to reinforce a specific phonics skill. The only materials kids need for the activities are crayons or colored pencils. To use, children follow the simple directions to complete each activity. You'll find several puzzle formats, as described below:

❄ **Hidden Pictures:** Children follow a color key to color different sections of these puzzles. When completed, a hidden picture is revealed.

❄ **Color-by-Sound Pictures:** A color key guides children in coloring different parts of a picture with specific colors. After they complete their picture, encourage children to check their work. Then invite them to fill in any uncolored areas in the colors of their choice.

❄ **Mazes:** To complete the mazes in this collection, children use specific colors to trace lines or color paths from a starting point to an end point.

❄ **Connect-the-Dots:** Children use what they know about phonics to connect the dots and reveal a mystery picture. When children complete the puzzle, invite them to color their picture.

Meeting the Language Arts Standards

Connections to the McREL Language Arts Standards

Mid-continent Research for Education and Learning (McREL), a nationally recognized nonprofit organization, has compiled and evaluated national and state standards—and proposed what teachers should provide for their K–2 students to grow proficient in language arts. This book's activities support the following standards:

Reading

Uses the general skills and strategies of the reading process including:

- Uses mental images based on pictures and print to aid in comprehension of text
- Uses basic elements of phonetic analysis (for example, common letter-sound relationships, beginning consonants, vowel sounds, blends, word patterns) to decode unknown words
- Uses basic elements of structural analysis, such as spelling patterns, to decode unknown words
- Uses self-correction strategies (searches for cues, identifies miscues, rereads)

Writing

Uses grammatical and mechanical conventions in written compositions including:

- Uses conventions of print in writing
- Uses conventions of spelling in written compositions (uses letter-sound relationships; spells basic short vowel, long vowel, and consonant blend patterns)

Source: Kendall, J. S., & Marzano, R. J. (2004). *Content knowledge: A compendium of standards and benchmarks for K–12 education.* Aurora, CO: Mid-continent Research for Education and Learning. Online database: http://www.mcrel.org/standards-benchmarks/

Connections to the Reading First Program

The activities in this book are also designed to support you in implementing the Reading First Program, authorized by the U.S. Department of Education's No Child Left Behind Act. The National Reading Panel has identified the five key areas of reading instruction as follows:

Phonemic Awareness

The ability to hear, identify, and manipulate phonemes—the sounds of spoken language

Phonics Development

Understanding the predictable relationship between phonemes and graphemes—the letters and spellings that represent those sounds in written language—helps readers recognize familiar words accurately and automatically and to decode unfamiliar words

Vocabulary Development

The ability to store information about the meanings and pronunciation of words necessary for communicating, including vocabulary for listening, speaking, reading, and writing

Fluency

The ability to read text accurately and quickly that allows readers to recognize words and comprehend at the same time

Comprehension

The ability to understand and gain meaning from material read

Source: *Guidance for the Reading First Program.* (U.S. Department of Education Office of Elementary and Secondary Education, 2002).

Choo Choo!

Name each picture. Write the letter it begins with.
Connect the dots in the order of your answers.
What picture did you make?

_____ 1.

_____ 2.

_____ 3.

_____ 4.

_____ 5.

_____ 6.

_____ 7.

_____ 8.

_____ 9.

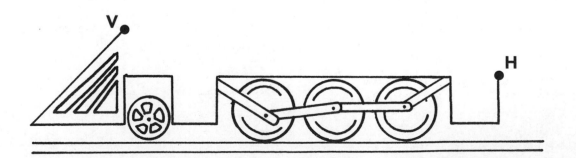

Name: _____ Date: _____

Time for Tea

Name each picture. Write the letter it begins with.
Connect the dots in the order of your answers.
What picture did you make?

_____ 1.   _____ 4.   _____ 7.

_____ 2.   _____ 5.   _____ 8.

_____ 3.   _____ 6.   _____ 9.

Name: _____   Date: _____

Jar of Jellybeans

If the word begins like	Color the jellybean
👑	Purple
⭐	Blue
📏	Red
🚐	Green
🕸️	Yellow

Color Key

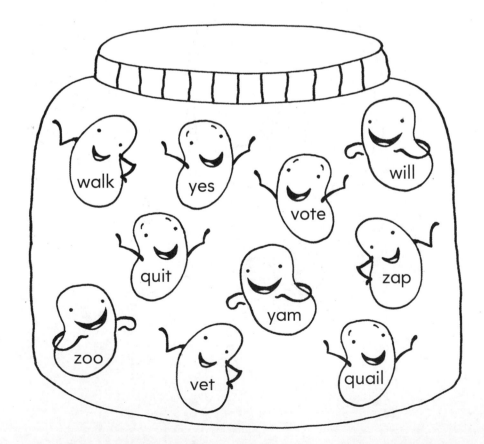

Name: _____   Date: _____

Through the Beehive

Help each bee get to the other side of the hive.
Name the item the bee is sitting on.
What letter does it begin with?

If a letter matches the beginning sound of	Color the space
🌿 (bushes)	Yellow
(fence)	Blue
(rock)	Orange

Color Key

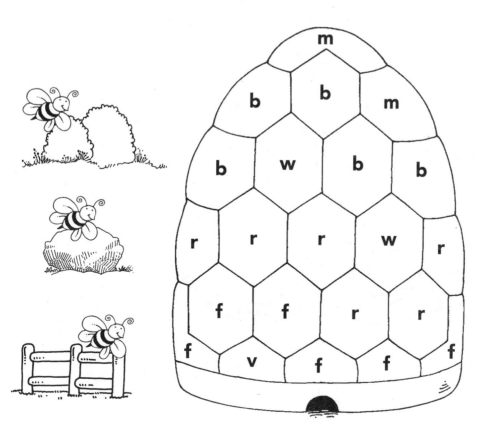

Ding Dong!

Name each picture. Write the letter it begins with.
Connect the dots in the order of your answers.
What picture did you make?

_____ 1.

_____ 2.

_____ 3.

_____ 4.

_____ 5.

_____ 6.

_____ 7.

_____ 8.

_____ 9.

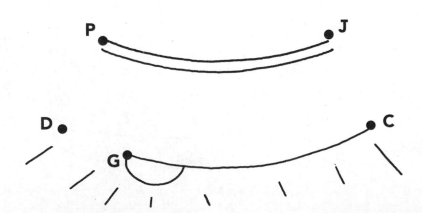

L · H

T ·   · N

P ·   · J

D ·   · C

G

Milk on the Move

Name each picture. Write the letter it ends with.
Connect the dots in the order of your answers.
What picture did you make?

_____ 1.   _____ 4.   _____ 7.

_____ 2.   _____ 5.   _____ 8.

_____ 3.   _____ 6.   _____ 9.

Home, Sweet Home

Name each picture. Write the letter it ends with.
Connect the dots in the order of your answers.
What picture did you make?

_____ 1.

_____ 2.

_____ 3.

_____ 4.

_____ 5.

_____ 6.

_____ 7.

_____ 8.

_____ 9.

x
•

g •   • t

b •——• r   s •   • d

n •   • k

12

Name: _____   Date: _____

Seven Swimmers

If the letter makes the sound at the end of	Color the space
🛁	Green
☕	Blue
🐟 (fish)	Yellow
10	Orange
☁️	Red

Color Key

Winter Wonderland

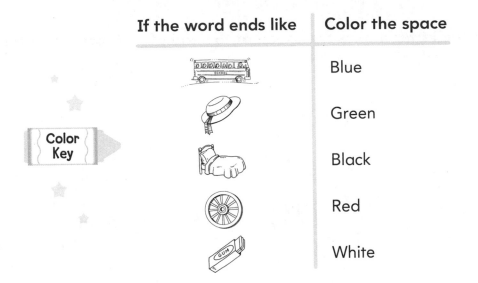

If the word ends like	Color the space
(bus)	Blue
(hat)	Green
(mitten)	Black
(fan)	Red
(gum)	White

Color Key

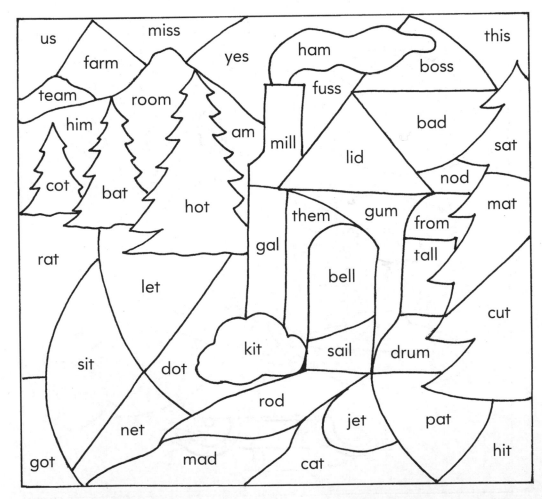

Name: _____ Date: _____

Ready to Roll

Name each picture. Write the letter it ends with.
Connect the dots in the order of your answers.
What picture did you make?

_____ 1.

_____ 2.

_____ 3.

_____ 4.

_____ 5.

_____ 6.

_____ 7.

_____ 8.

_____ 9.

f

s

m

g

k

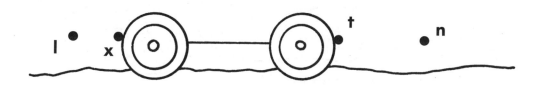

l

x

t

n

To the Beach

Help the crab get to the beach.
Find each word that has the same vowel sound as ⌇.
Color that space red.

web	yam	van	bad
red	that	wet	cab
bell	tan	clap	less
pet	fed	sad	jet
hat	ten	ran	step
map	rack	bag	men

Hippity-Hop

Find each word that has the same vowel sound as .
Color that space brown.
Color the other spaces blue.

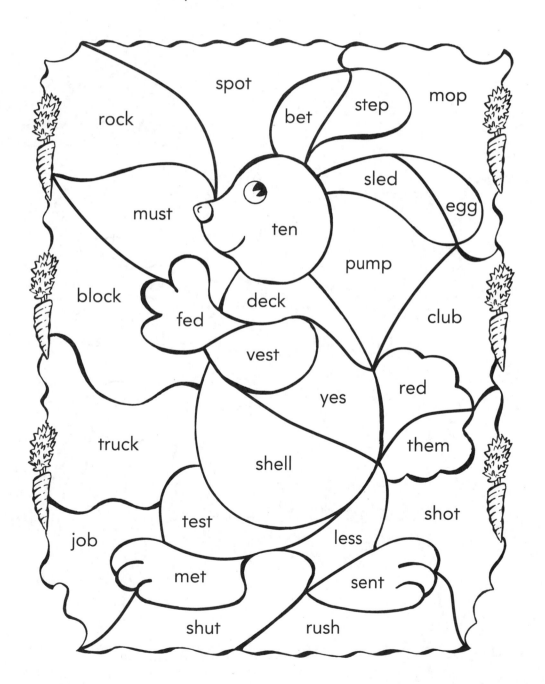

Name: _____ Date: _____

Sea Shopper

Help the dolphin get to the Sea Shop.
Find each word that has the same vowel sound as .
Color that space green.

fish   win   pill   him   crop

list   desk   log   tent

pet   this   clip   left   rod

rid   lift   cot   went

Across the Pond

Help the frog get to the lily pad.
Find each word that has the same vowel sound as .
Color that space brown.

box	rock	hot	bed	sun
fan	hill	pond	tap	him
cub	mop	log	cup	ran
lid	dock	yes	pit	tug
ram	job	bat	nod	chop
best	hop	jog	lock	set

Looking for Flowers

Help the ladybug get to the flowers.
Find each word that has the same vowel sound as .
Color that space orange.

must	catch	fed	wag	rest
mug	step	pup	jump	buzz
tub	such	drum	past	much
jam	went	bath	bell	sum
duck	plus	cut	run	up

Phonics Picture Puzzles for Little Learners © 2011 by Scholastic Teaching Resources

Pizza Party!

Sound out each short vowel on the pizza.

If the vowel matches the sound you hear in	Color the space
airplane	Orange
tree	Brown
STOP	Red
sun	Yellow

Color Key

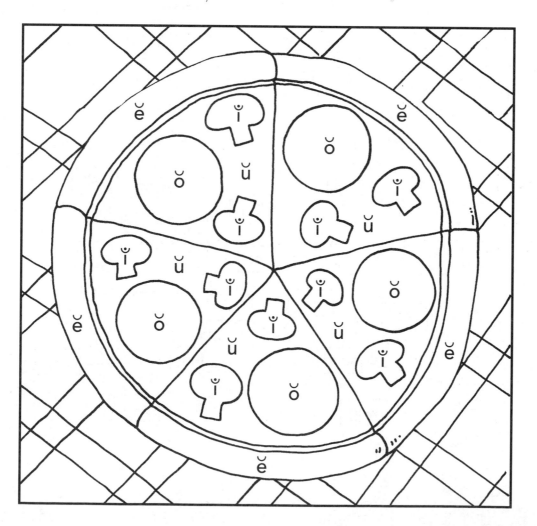

Falling Down

Help each leaf get to its basket using a word path.

If the word has the same vowel sound as	Color the box and trace the line
(bag)	Brown
(foot)	Orange
(pig)	Red
(nut)	Yellow

Color Key

set — red — big — mug — rat — will — hid
than — men — fell
sit — but — ham — fun — rub
sand — last — king — peg — jump

ă ĭ ĕ ŭ

22

Happy Robot

If the word has the same vowel sound as	Color the space
(inline skate)	Purple
(bicycle)	Yellow

Color Key

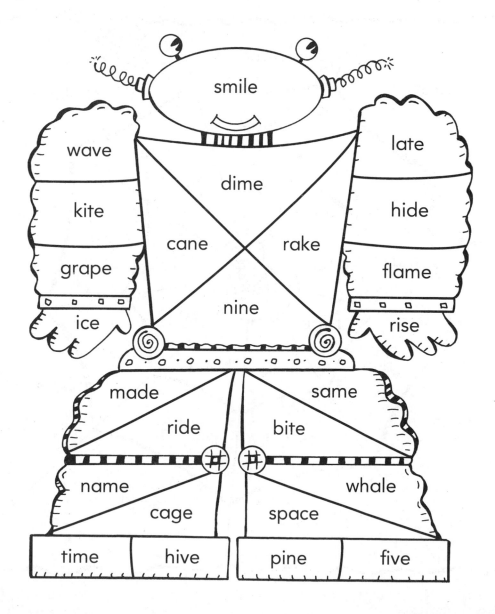

smile
wave
late
dime
kite
hide
cane   rake
grape
flame
ice
nine
rise
made   same
ride   bite
name   whale
cage   space
time   hive   pine   five

Spider and Fly

Silent e

If the word has the same vowel sound as	Color the space
Color Key 🖍️ 🦴 (bone)	Yellow
🎵 (flute)	Orange

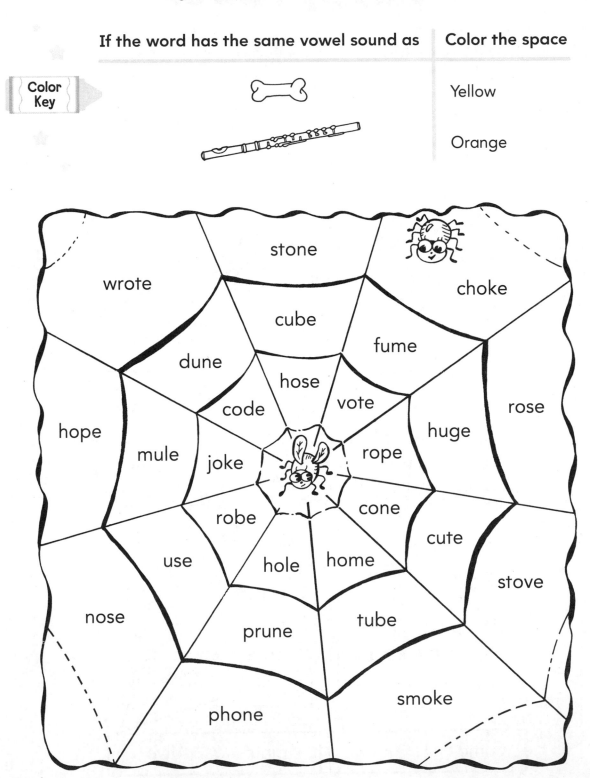

Words in the web:
stone, wrote, choke, cube, fume, dune, hose, vote, rose, code, hope, huge, mule, joke, rope, robe, cone, cute, use, hole, home, stove, nose, prune, tube, phone, smoke

Bubbles Everywhere!

If the word has a	Color the bubble
Long-*a* sound	Blue
Long-*i* sound	Green
Long-*o* sound	Purple
Long-*u* sound	Red

Color Key

tune

name

dice

mule

five

bone

rope

late

white

globe

brake

cube

shine

zone

tape

close

tube

flute

scale

made

like

side

25

Friendly Fire-Breather

	If the word has a	Color the space
Color Key	Long-*a* sound	Yellow
	Long-*i* sound	Green
	Long-*o* sound	Blue
	Long-*u* sound	Red

Alien Artists

If the word has the same vowel sound as	Color the space
Color Key	
(broom) and (snail)	Purple
(feet) and (peach)	Orange

meat

beach

tree

mail

seed

paint

bean

play

jeep

flea

say

rain

day

paid

feel

wait

bee

may

tail

sea

read

sweep

leaf

27

Quilt Star

If the word has the same vowel sound as	Color the space
Color Key ➤ [sailboat] and [foot]	Yellow
[suit/coat] and [glue]	Blue

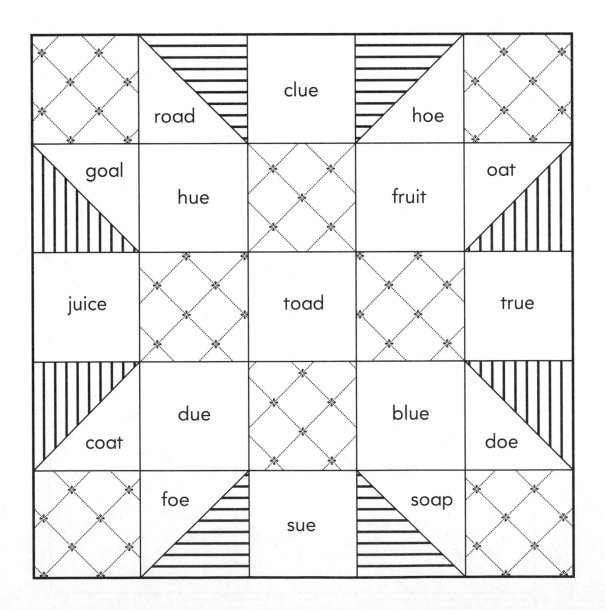

road · clue · hoe

goal · hue · fruit · oat

juice · toad · true

coat · due · blue · doe

foe · sue · soap

Sparkling Stone

Name each picture. Fill in the missing vowel pair.
Connect the dots in the order of your answers.
What picture did you make?

h __ __ **1.**   t __ __ **4.**   sh __ __ p **7.**

l __ __ f **2.**   n __ __ l **5.**   tr __ __ **8.**

fr __ __ t **3.**   g __ __ t **6.**    gl __ __ **9.**

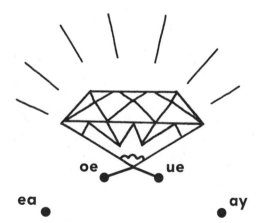

oe   ue

ea

ay

ui

ee

ie

oa

ai

Finned Friend

Name each picture. Fill in the missing vowel pair.
Connect the dots in the order of your answers.
What picture did you make?

j _ _ **1.**   t _ _ **4.** 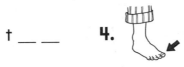   s _ _ t **7.**

p _ _ **2.**   b _ _ n **5.**   t _ _ th **8.**

bl _ _ **3.**   ch _ _ n **6.**    r _ _ d **9.**

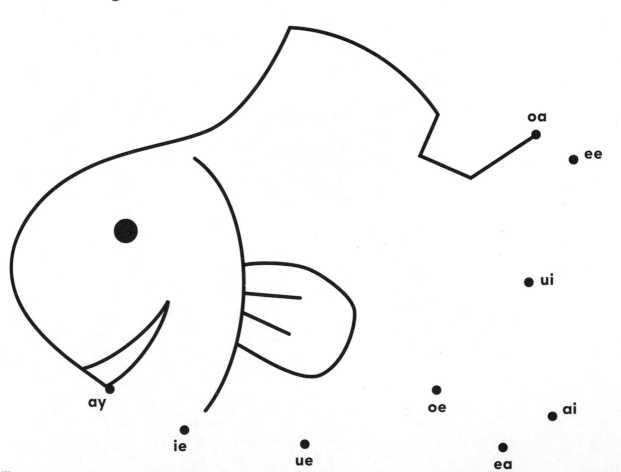

oa

ee

ui

ay

oe

ai

ie

ue

ea

Space Travel

If the word has the same vowel sound as	Color the star
(clown)	Orange
(boy)	Yellow

Color Key

now

house

coin

brown

joy

count

soil

soy

gown

round

join

toy

Where's My Bone?

Help each dog get to its bone using a word path.

If the word has the same vowel sound as	Color the box and trace the line
Color Key	Blue
	Red
	Green

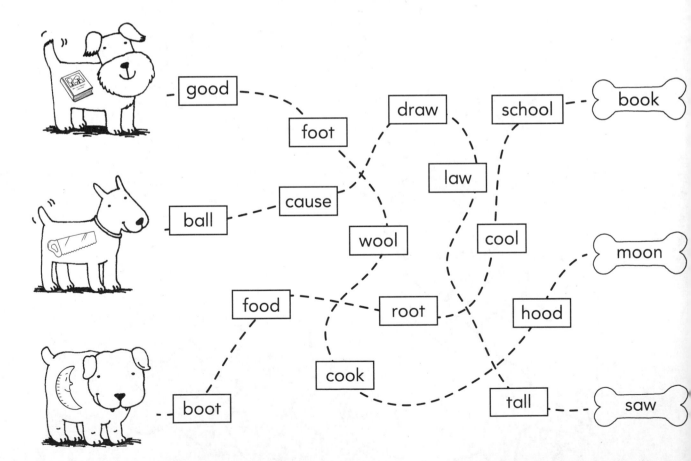

Phonics Picture Puzzles for Little Learners © 2011 by Scholastic Teaching Resources

Name: _____ Date: _____

Turtle Topper

Color the scales on the turtle's shell.
Find each word that has the same vowel sound as ☐.
Color that scale green. Color all of the other scales brown.

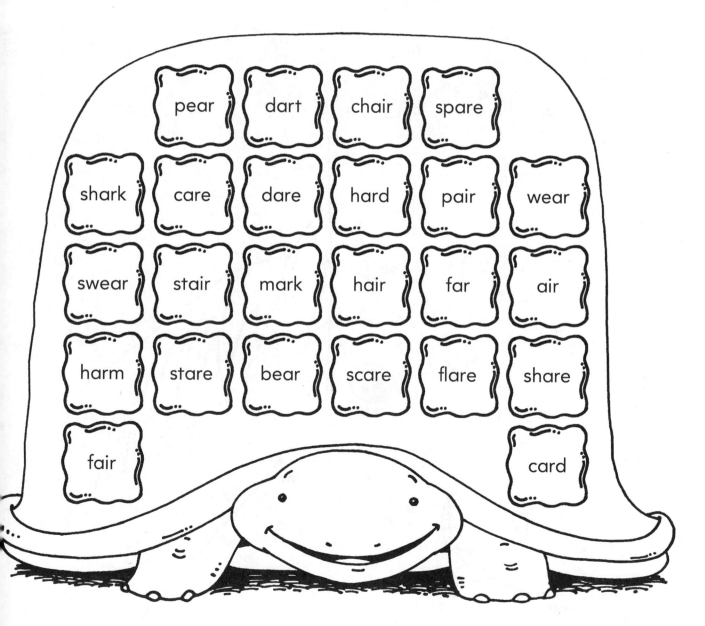

pear · dart · chair · spare

shark · care · dare · hard · pair · wear

swear · stair · mark · hair · far · air

harm · stare · bear · scare · flare · share

fair · card

A Neighborly Smile

Name each picture. Fill in the missing vowel pairs.
Connect the dots in the order of your answers.
What picture did you make?

h __ __ se **1.**   sp __ __ n **4.**   t __ __ s **6.**

str __ __ **2.**   cr __ __ n **5.**   l __ __ nch **7.**

c __ __ n **3.**

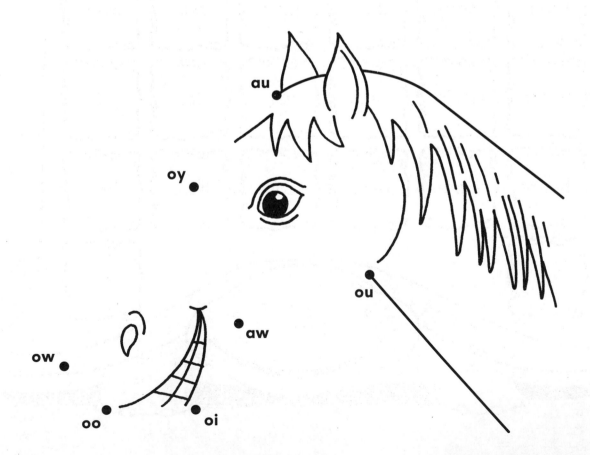

Top of the Wall

Help the cat get to the top of the wall.
Find each word that has the same vowel sound as  and .
Color that space green.

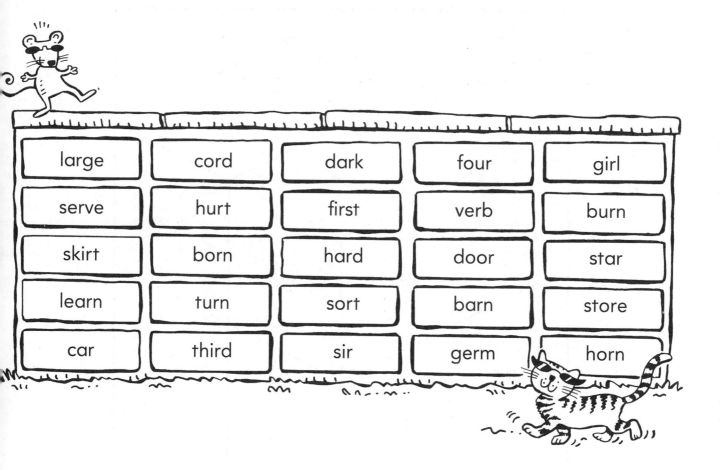

large	cord	dark	four	girl
serve	hurt	first	verb	burn
skirt	born	hard	door	star
learn	turn	sort	barn	store
car	third	sir	germ	horn

Puzzle Cube

R-Controlled Vowels

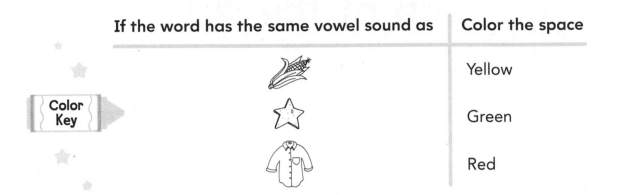

If the word has the same vowel sound as	Color the space
(corn)	Yellow
(star)	Green
(shirt)	Red

Color Key

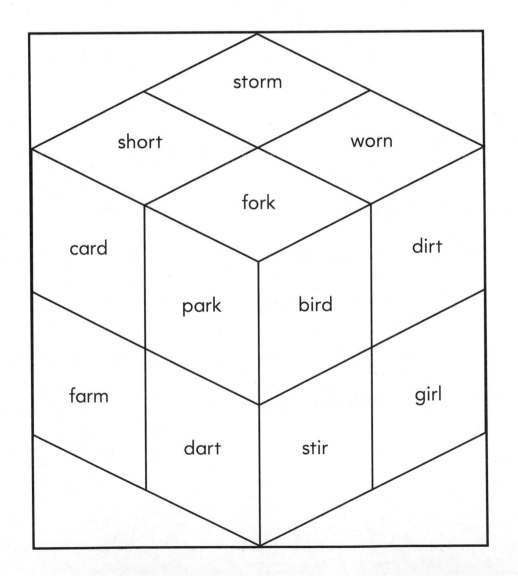

storm

short   worn

fork

card   dirt

park   bird

farm   girl

dart   stir

Name: _____ Date: _____

Up, Up, and Away!

If the word begins like	Color the space
A (block)	Blue
(frisbee)	Red
(flag)	Yellow
(glove)	Green
(slide)	Purple

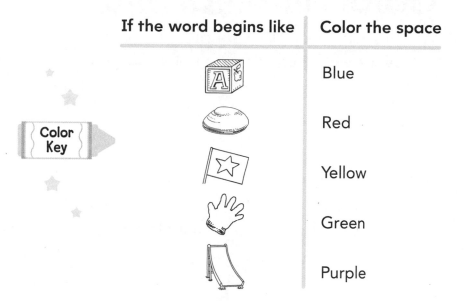

Color Key

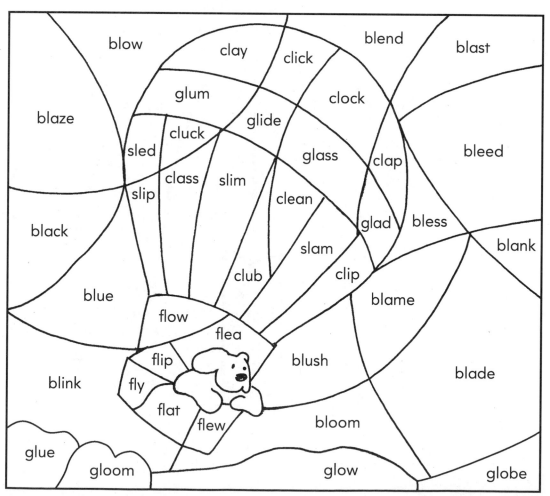

blow clay click blend blast

glum clock

blaze glide

cluck

sled glass clap bleed

class slim clean

slip

black glad bless

slam blank

club clip

blue blame

flow

flea

flip blush

blink fly blade

flat

flew bloom

glue

gloom glow globe

Colorful Umbrella

If the word begins like	Color the space
 (drum)	Red
 (bread)	Yellow
 (tree)	Purple

Color
Key

drag

drop

brick

treat

dream

brand

truck

bring

trap

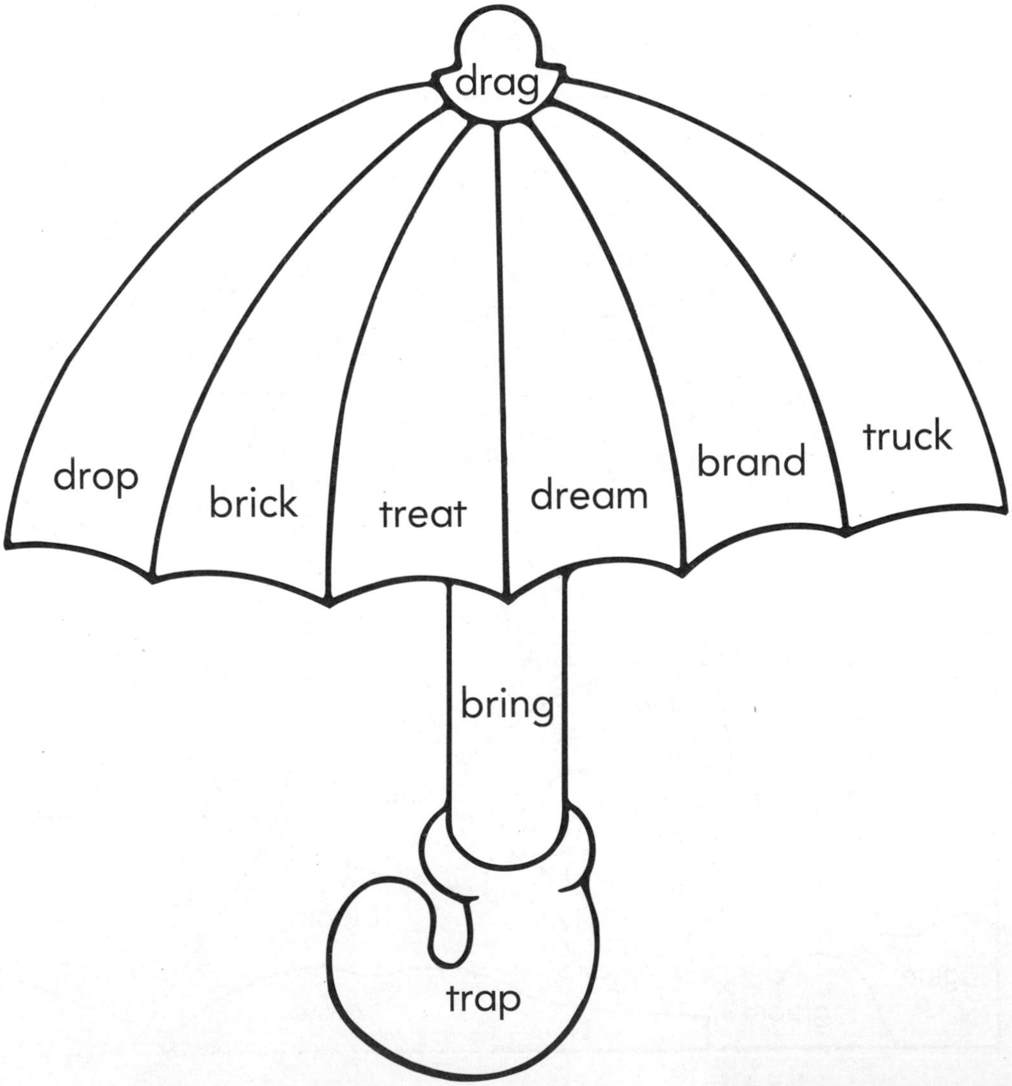

Flutter By

If the word begins like	Color the space
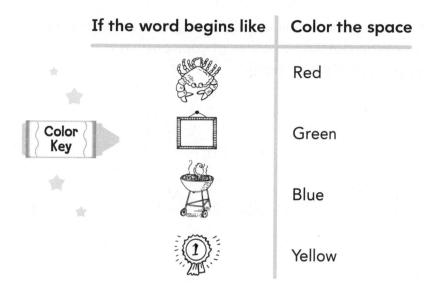	Red
	Green
	Blue
	Yellow

Color Key

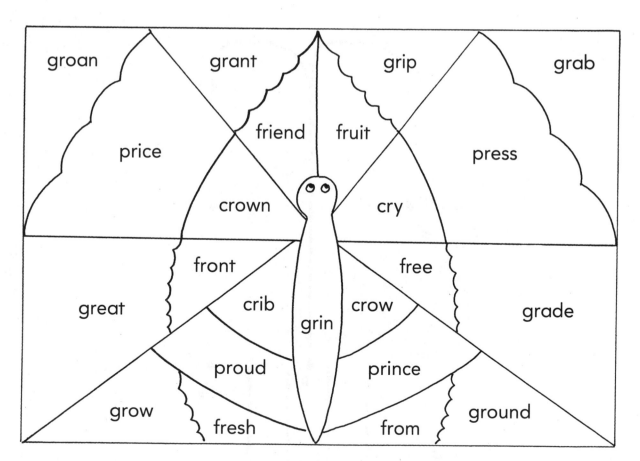

groan

grant

grip

grab

friend

fruit

price

press

crown

cry

front

free

great

crib

crow

grade

grin

proud

prince

grow

from

ground

fresh

Cool Treat

Name each picture. Fill in the missing two-letter blend.
Connect the dots in the order of your answers.
What picture did you make?

__ __ im **1.**

__ __ unk **4.**

__ __ ale **6.**

__ __ oon **2.**

__ __ ake **5.**

__ __ ove **7.**

__ __ oke **3.**

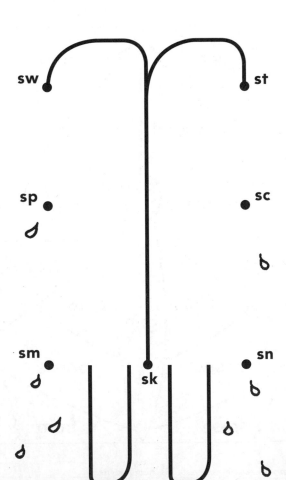

sw

st

sp

sc

sm

sk

sn

Love Struck

Name each picture. Fill in the missing two-letter blend.
Connect the dots in the order of your answers.
What picture did you make?

__ __ ug **1.**

__ __ own **2.**

__ __ ing **3.**

__ __ uck **4.**

__ __ ow **5.**

__ __ ass **6.**

__ __ eep **7.**

__ __ arf **8.**

__ __ og **9.**

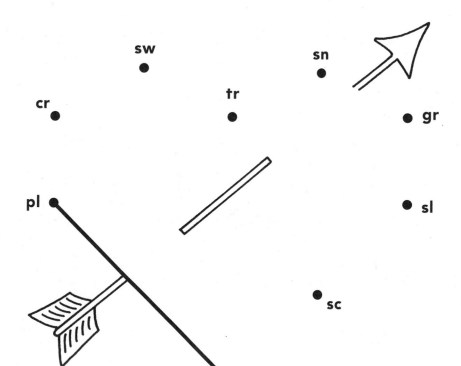

sw •

cr •

tr •

sn •

gr •

pl •

sl •

sc •

fr •

Caterpillar Crawlers

If the word begins like	Color the space
(chair)	Purple
(shell)	Red
(hand)	Green

Color Key

ship · thaw · chop · thin · child · third · shape

thing · thorn · shoe · shade · chin · cheep · thick

chew · chalk · chick · thank · short · shave · shirt

Name: _____ Date: _____

Finding Mom

Help each chick get to its mother.

If the word begins like	Color the space
Color Key ▶	
(branch)	Yellow
(whale)	Red

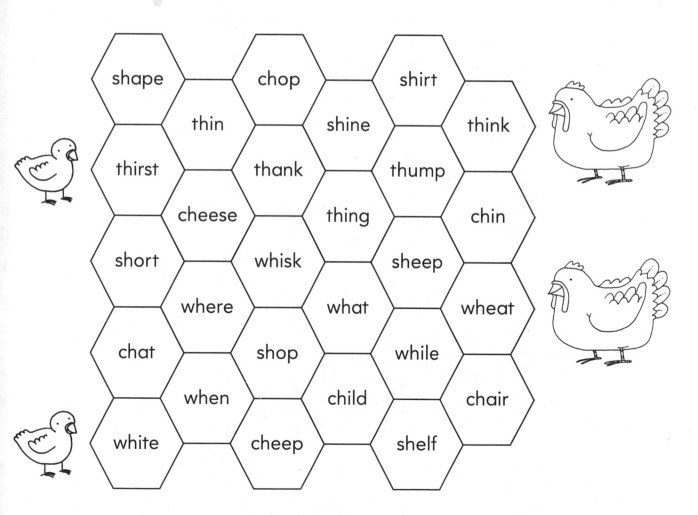

shape   chop   shirt
thin   shine   think
thirst   thank   thump
cheese   thing   chin
short   whisk   sheep
where   what   wheat
chat   shop   while
when   child   chair
white   cheep   shelf

Light Up!

If the word ends like	Color the space
🐟	Yellow
🦷	Orange
🛋	Green

Color Key

watch

mouth

lunch

dish

bush

with

cloth

inch

wash

path

fresh

hatch

Answer Key

Color Abbreviations

R = Red	G = Green	Br = Brown
B = Blue	O = Orange	Bk = Black
Y = Yellow	P = Purple	W = White

Choo Choo, page 6

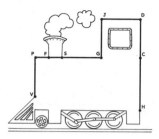

1. V
2. P
3. F
4. S
5. G
6. J
7. D
8. C
9. H

Time for Tea, page 7

1. M
2. B
3. N
4. L
5. R
6. Z
7. W
8. T
9. K

Jar of Jellybeans, page 8

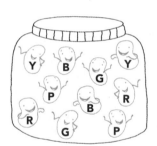

Through the Beehive, page 9

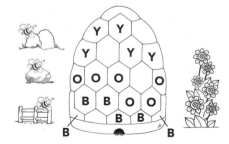

Ding Dong!, page 10

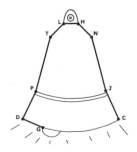

1. G
2. D
3. P
4. T
5. L
6. H
7. N
8. J
9. C

Milk on the Move, page 11

1. p
2. g
3. b
4. k
5. f
6. n
7. x
8. r
9. l

Home, Sweet Home, page 12

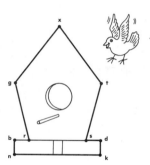

1. r
2. g
3. x
4. t
5. s
6. d
7. k
8. n
9. b

Seven Swimmers, page 13

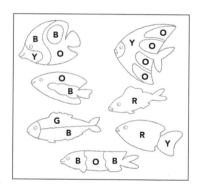

Winter Wonderland, page 14

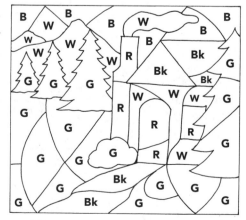

Ready to Roll, page 15

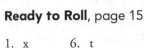

1.	x	6.	t
2.	l	7.	n
3.	m	8.	s
4.	g	9.	f
5.	k		

To the Beach,
page 16

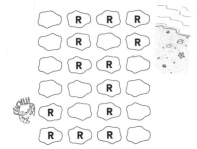

Hippity-Hop,
page 17

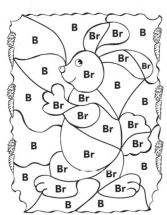

Sea Shopper,
page 18

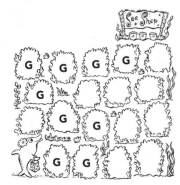

Across the Pond,
page 19

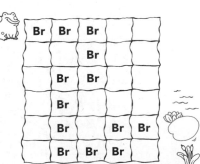

Looking for Flowers,
page 20

Pizza Party!,
page 21

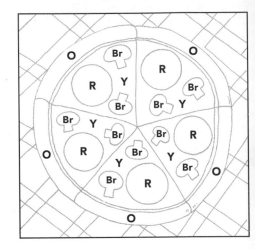

Falling Down, page 22

- Students should use brown to color the boxes with the following words, then trace the line that connects these boxes: *rat, than, ham, sand, last*

- Students should use orange to color the boxes with the following words, then trace the line that connects these boxes: *set, red, men, fell, peg*

- Students should use red to color the boxes with the following words, then trace the line that connects these boxes: *hid, will, big, sit, king*

- Students should use yellow to color the boxes with the following words, then trace the line that connects these boxes: *mug, but, fun, rub, jump*

Happy Robot,
page 23

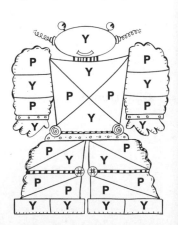

Spider and Fly,
page 24

Bubbles Everywhere!,
page 25

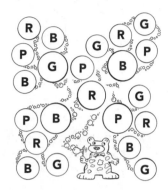

Friendly Fire-Breather,
page 26

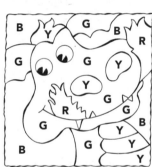

Alien Artists,
page 27

Quilt Star,
page 28

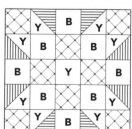

Sparkling Stone, page 29

1. oe
2. ea
3. ui
4. ie
5. ai
6. oa
7. ee
8. ay
9. ue

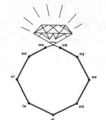

Finned Friend, page 30

1. ay
2. ie
3. ue
4. oe
5. ea
6. ai
7. ui
8. ee
9. oa

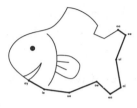

Space Travel, page 31

Where's My Bone?, page 32

- Students should use blue to color the boxes with the following words, then trace the line that connects these boxes: *good, foot, wool, cook, hood*

- Students should use red to color the boxes with the following words, then trace the line that connects these boxes: *ball, cause, draw, law, tall*

- Students should use green to color the boxes with the following words, then trace the line that connects these boxes: *boot, food, root, cool, school*

Turtle Topper,
page 33

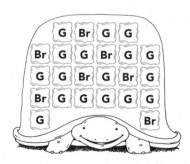

A Neighborly Smile, page 34

1. ou
2. aw
3. oi
4. oo
5. ow
6. oy
7. au

Top of the Wall, page 35

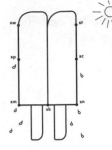

Cool Treat, page 40

1. sw
2. sp
3. sm
4. sk
5. sn
6. sc
7. st

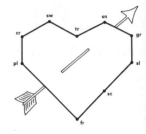

Puzzle Cube, page 36

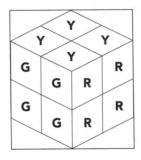

Love Struck, page 41

1. pl
2. cr
3. sw
4. tr
5. sn
6. gr
7. sl
8. sc
9. fr

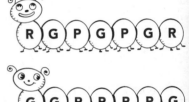

Up, Up, and Away!, page 37

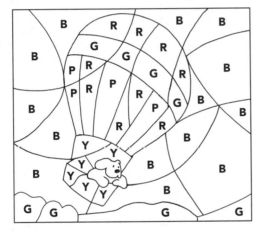

Caterpillar Crawlers, page 42

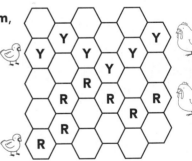

Colorful Umbrella, page 38

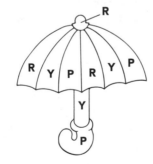

Finding Mom, page 43

Flutter By, page 39

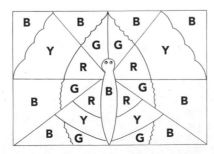

Light Up!, page 44